THE LITTLE BOOK OF

A

As
be...
from
around
the
country

ED WEST

Crombie Jardine
PUBLISHING LIMITED

13 Nonsuch Walk, Cheam, Surrey, SM2 7LG
www.crombiejardine.com

Published by Crombie Jardine Publishing Limited
First edition, 2005

ISBN 1-905102-41-0

Designed by 'Mr Stiffy'
Printed & bound in the United Kingdom by
William Clowes Ltd, Beccles, Suffolk

Contents

Introduction: WE'RE ASBOLUTELY FABULOUS!

BRITAIN HAS GONE ASBO MAD...

This year there will be an estimated 24 million incidents of anti-social behaviour in the UK. that's 66,000 a day or almost one every second. No wonder that it's impossible to open a newspaper without reading about an Asbo handed out to some ne'er do well. persistent thief or

nightmare neighbour. Anti-social
is the buzzword of 2005.

What is an Asbo?

1. An Anti-social behaviour order
is a local authority measure
designed to prevent an individual
or group from travelling to
certain areas, wearing clothes
likely to aide criminal disguise,
or behaving in a manner
'likely to cause harassment,
alarm or distress.' Anyone
over ten years old is liable.

2. A teenage rapscallion, generally of low intelligence and ambition and likely to be dressed in a hooded top bearing the name of an American town he'll never visit and a sport he doesn't even understand, who's been issued with the local authority measure as described on p.7.

The orders were introduced to England and Wales by the Crime and Disorder Act in 1998, and since that time over 4,000 have been handed out. Northern Ireland introduced them in 2003 and Scotland the following year, while the Irish Republic plans to follow suit. Because they are civil orders, Asbos are dealt with by a magistrate not a judge, and require less proof than a criminal conviction, but they can carry a maximum prison sentence of five

years if broken. The minimum
length of an Asbo is two years.

Although usually given for abuse,
threats, noise pollution and
harassment, you can find yourself
on the end of an Asbo for the
strangest of reasons. For example,
failing to cut down hedges over
6ft 6in and having a noisy dog are
Asbo offences, while Mansfield
council plans to bring them into
schools for uncontrollable children.

The list of infringements also keeps growing: under proposals by Trading Standards bosses, dodgy builders and plumbers, cheating estate agents and doorstep salesmen will also be affected. Over 100,000 people are ripped off in this way, and according to statisticians who work out these sorts of arbitrary financial figures, it costs the economy £1bn annually.

More strangely, you can find
yourself in trouble for answering
the door in your underwear,
having your gang name shaved
into your head, trying to commit
suicide or any number of odd
reasons discussed more later on.

And despite criticisms about Asbos
from the EU, human rights group
Liberty and probation bodies,
the government has pledged to
increase the number issued out to

6,000 a year. So you better learn
to love your neighbour, or else.

BRITAIN'S MOST ANTI-SOCIAL

Here are the people the Asbo was made for: to call this lot bad apples would be doing even the most rancid of ciders a disservice. This bunch is so rotten their mothers probably put their names down for Wormwood Scrubs when they were born.

THE REAL VICKY POLLARD

One Tyneside teenager turned out to be a tabloid dream come true earlier this year, earning the nickname 'the real Vicky Pollard', and not just for her ubiquitous tracksuit, Romford facelift and total lack of erudition. The 19-year-old inspired 111 complaints from neighbours, and had entertained

the police on 25 occasions, for
offences ranging from tying a naked
teenager to a lamppost to threatening
someone with a hammer. But she
sure could throw a party – kids
as young as ten years old were
regularly seen boozing it up at her
flat, and she even held moped and
motorbike races outside. She was
eventually sent down to the nick for
a three-stretch. Three days, that is.

FEAR AND LOATHING IN SWANAGE

After 20 arrests and 16 convictions in four years, one teenager from Dorset received her first Asbo last year, with newspapers claiming she was responsible for 85% of all crime in her hometown of Swanage. The 17-year-old's reign of terror included setting fire to a ladies' toilet, and notching up 73 abusive tirades against staff in an amusement arcade in 23 days. When thrown out, the young lady told the 54-year-old female owner: 'Fucking come out, you fat slag.'

JUST THE ONE THEN

On a relatively lighter note, a Peterborough drunk received an Asbo barring him from drinking in the city centre after spending 12 nights in police cells in five months. The 51-year-old has already breached it twice at the time of going to press, on one occasion ringing the police to inform them he was drunk. He claims to have slept on every park bench in

Peterborough. and once even resorted to a coffin in an undertaker's parlour.

MIND WHERE YOU GO

The youngest Asbo case in Middlesbrough is a 13-year-old involved in 120 incidents. After making over a crime century. he was banned from drinking in public. taking illegal drugs. and landed a geographical ban that allows him to visit his patch only to see his grandmother. and visit from 2.55pm to 3.30pm, but only using the most awkward of routes. Perhaps he'll coin a phrase – 'As the Asbo walks' being the opposite to 'as the crow flies'.

ONE-WOMAN LICENSING LAWS

A drunken hag who punched a man so hard in August 2004 that he needed hospital treatment was banned from every pub, hotel and nightclub in Conwy, North Wales, for the next five years. The 48-year-old also can't

consume booze in public anywhere
in Britain (including gardens)
and has to stay indoors between
9pm and 6am for six months.

NEVER MEET YOUR HEROES

A 15-year-old from Mansfield had an
interest in the fire brigade that went
beyond healthy, and ended up banned
from entering telephone kiosks. As
well as making hoax calls, he was
accused of assaulting police officers,
committing public order offences and

causing criminal damage. His social worker stated in court: 'He loves the fire service and visits them whenever he can. He wants to see the firemen in their shiny uniforms, hear the engine and sirens and see the flashing lights.' We all need our heroes!

ASBOS FOR HOBOS

Every area has its local tramp, but Middlesbrough town centre was the unfortunate home of a supergroup of six, who currently are awaiting a group Asbo instruction. The hobos are accused of harassing shoppers, and even leaving a syringe in a busy shopping centre. And to think that Bluewater gets annoyed over a little hooded top!

NOT SO CLEVER

A young art enthusiast is one of a growing number of teenagers banned from carrying spray paint, after the 19-year-old Geordie's tag, 'Clever Sever' was traced back to him, though admittedly he had increased the likelihood of this by using the walls of his own house to practise it. It didn't help his case that when police came to raid his home, they found 20 Ecstasy pills hidden in his PlayStation.

GRAND THEFT ASBO

An Exeter man was banned from every car park in Devon after being named as one of the city's top three car criminals. But the 25-year-old failed to stick to his order, which was given for breaking into 28 cars and causing £11,000 damage — an average of £400 per vehicle.

PUTTING THE C*** IN SCUNTHORPE

The lawyer representing a Scunthorpe teen tearaway told the court: 'I have to accept that the conduct of my client has been questionable.' His client was accused of harassing an off-duty policeman outside his home, being present as objects were thrown at a postie, threatening witnesses, making threats to kill, criminal damage and assaulting a police officer. After being accused of involvement in 28 different criminal incidents over the previous eight months, she was banned from acting like an obnoxious arsehole for two years.

MALL BRATS

As if shopping centres aren't awful enough, Bolton girls aged 16 and 14, made their local mall a great deal worse by setting fire to bins.

switching off escalators, abusing staff, using racist language, spitting at people, throwing a lit cigarette at a security guard, and fighting each other. The 14-year-old repeatedly harassed staff at Bolton police station, despite her dad being a former PC.

4 GO MAD IN YORKSHIRE

Four patients at a mental hospital were forced to sign a contract agreeing to behave well after whiling away a lazy afternoon on a bowling green drinking, littering and vomiting. Next time you're in Yorkshire and some people drinking in public say 'we're mad, us', they might be telling the truth this time.

THE STELLA KID STUMBLES INTO TOWN

A lager-lover who led a gang assault on a man in Epsworth ended up with a Wild West-style three-year ban from the Lincolnshire town. The court scene could have been

straight out of a John Wayne film.
apart from the clause allowing him
to visit his social worker mother. and
the fact that his lawyer pointed out
he'd drunk 'about 20 cans of Stella'.

LEEDS' LIL' RASCAL

A 10-year-old Leeds boy was too
young to be prosecuted for any of
his crimes – burglary. glue sniffing.
assault and throwing a scooter at
a packed bus – so instead he was
banned from four districts of the city

and from meeting 17 different kids.
His doting mother told the paper: 'I
know he's a cheeky so-and-so.' Bless.

RESIDENT EVIL

A Romford family were thrown out
of their home after making life so
unpleasant for those around them
that a 56-year-old disabled neighbour
had to hire a team of security
guards. The family – a woman, her
boyfriend, her two teenage daughters,
and their two children, left broken

furniture, old TVs and toys in their back garden. Another neighbour, a mother-of-three, had to flee after being attacked by the nightmare woman and her two daughters – they kicked in her front door and battered her with household objects as she held her five-year-old son to her chest. When people in Romford say, 'lock up your daughters', it's probably for your sake as much as theirs.

JUNKIE'S SUPERMARKET SWEEP

A real-life Nick Cotton from Chorley, Lancashire but with less of the charm, got an eight-month prison sentence and five-year ban from the town centre after burgling a Boots store and running off with a load of razors. But he wasn't fussy — as well as the Boots job, he stole PlayStation games from Tesco, aftershave from Debenhams and dolls from Woolworths. Either he was prepared to nick anything, or had some devious A-Team-style plan up his sleeve. Probably the former.

ASBOS – A BREAKDOWN ON THE STATS OF SOCIETY'S BREAKDOWN

Almost 4,000 Asbos have been issued, and the Asbo capital of Britain is Manchester – the city council has handed out 474 since January 2004, meaning a Mancunian is five times more likely to be Asboed than a Scouser and six times more than a Brummie. Manchester council's website even boasts that it 'now leads the UK in the use of Asbos'. At the other end of the scale, Geordies seem especially reluctant to get on the Asbo bandwagon, with all North-East councils handing out a tenth of that of the West Midlands.

The Asbo premier league. 2000-2005 season:

1. Greater Manchester - 608

2. Greater London - 364

3. West Yorkshire - 299

4. West Midlands - 271

5. Lancashire - 146.

The numbers are rising – Birmingham gave out 23 in 2002, 69 the following year and over 100 in 2004.

If a council wants you to have one, the chances are they will get their way. Of the 2,497 orders sought before April 2004, only 42 were refused – that's a success rate of over 98%.

The image of the typical Asbo
case as a hoodie-wearing
Eminem fan is not far off:

45% have been
against children.

50% involved noise nuisance.

25% involved booze
or drug addiction.

On average, an Asbo costs
the authorities £5,000 to
serve from start to finish.

50% of all Asbos are
breached, though the Scots
seem especially unfazed
by the order – north of
the Tweed the breach
rate rises to 67%.

Aside from Asbos, there
are several types of orders
that an aspiring jailbird
can pick up:

Acceptable behaviour agreements

Described as Asbo lite and
sometimes called Abas, these
are voluntary contracts
between a tearaway and
local council, promising
to behave in future or get
kicked out of his/her home.

*

Parenting orders

A counselling course reserved for the type of parents who likes to blame the council, police, CIA or freemasons for 'victimising' their little rascals.

*

Penalty notice for disorder

For minor anti-social actions, and involving a fine given by a policeman or community support officer, ranging from £30 to £80.

*

Dispersal order

Issued in January 2004 to stop teens hanging around in a menacing way, and forcing them out of an area - 418 have been given out in so-called 'Dispersal Zones'.

*

For issues less serious, such as a dispute between neighbours, a mediation group called UNITE will do the proverbial 'calm down' before it gets any more serious.

*

Alternatively, you can also be nominated for an Outstanding Behaviour Special Award, which carries a £250 prize. Although to be consistent, if you do something nice again with the next two years, the council should book you into a free hotel.

*

NEIGHBOURS FROM HELL

It's a phrase that rolls effortlessly off the tongue of newspaper reporters, and we may all think we've had some, but these 'neighbours from hell' are so unpleasant even Satan

himself wouldn't want them next
door, keeping him up all night with
Motorhead concert noise levels.
Here are some of the worst...

BAD VIBRATIONS

A 47-year-old rock nut kept neighbours
awake with 3ft-tall professional
speakers for seven years, his reign
of terror ending in a five-year Asbo
and the temporary confiscation of
guitars, drums, an amp and some rare

cymbals. The heavy metal fan, who said he was attempting to emulate his hero Brian Wilson of the Beach Boys, was finally done for his metal madness by Flintshire council. Not the type of supernatural force that usually appears in heavy metal's fantasy-driven lyrics.

NOT SO GIRL NEXT DOOR

A court case in April 2004 was livened up by a Derby woman's 470-page diary, in which she chronicled her feelings for the woman next door.

generally verging on loathing. The diarist was a victim of a woman given the title 'ultimate neighbour from hell' by the papers, and the journal included intimidation, abuse and the constant dropping off and fixing of cars. With some clever editing the paperback could become a bestseller.

EVERYONE DESERVES A 56TH CHANCE

An Aberdeen nuisance neighbour was only kicked out of his council house after ignoring an Asbo 55 times. Still, because the law ensures that he's entitled to stay in the area, the 55-year-old was just moved around the corner.

RENT BOYO GAGGED

A man in Colwyn Bay, North Wales, must be Britain's ultimate landlord from hell, after he was issued with an Asbo to restrict him from being insulting, offensive, threatening or using intimidating language or behaviour towards his tenants in a public place. Strangely, they also banned him from referring to himself as 'Rachman', the notorious 1960s slum landlord of Notting Hill who treated the people he rented to so badly that his name inspired the dictionary entry Rachmanism: 'Landlords buying up slums to fill with immigrants at extortionate rent.'

CLASS GIVEN FROSTY RECEPTION

It can be a nightmare when a new business opens next to your home.

with all the accompanying noise and traffic, so many of us will understand why a man in Hamilton conducted a hate campaign of swearing, shouting and threatening customers – from next door's children's nursery. A total of 19 people made complaints against the man, and even fellow opponents to the nursery's opening were eventually alienated by his combative style. He now has to be nice to parents and staff.

FIGHT FOR YOUR RIGHTS ... TO PARK

A 55-year-old man from Portsmouth
was banned from parking in
a disabled bay after refusing
to move from his 86-year-old
neighbour's clearly marked parking
space. When she complained, he
called her 'village pond life' and
her daughter 'a fat midget.'

SPEAK NO DRIVEL

A charity worker was given an Asbo

after a seven-year hate campaign against neighbours, banning him from, among other things, making accusations of drug-dealing. The man, who worked for Age Concern, was also alleged to have headbutted a man, kicked a 15-year-old, and called a woman a 'whore'. The 50-year-old is now not allowed to use the phrases 'council scum', 'fairy', 'druggie', 'army boy' or 'trash' — except perhaps in reference to actual refuse.

LIVING NEXT DOOR TO MALICE

A household in Dunfermline this year became the first family in Scotland to be banned from their own home after their teenaged son held a series of rowdy parties. Get-togethers involving teens are usually lively affairs, but neighbours became uneasy about the frequent outdoor knife fights that would result. A newspaper reported on their overgrown lawn piled high with smashed glass and rubbish, their living room furnished with plastic garden chairs, and plates laden with cigarette ash. The final touch was provided by a charred garden gnome by the entrance. Still, in the unlikely event of the son ever making it to university, he should fit in perfectly.

SALESMAN'S CHARM OFFENSIVE

A former conservatory salesman with a conviction for blackmail subjected his neighbours to a colourful catalogue of abuse. The County Durham man used poetic phrases such as 'pathetic twat', 'witch' and 'manipulative bitch' when addressing neighbours and told one man, 'I can be a psychopath. I will make your life hell.' Even less sympathetic was his reaction when he reversed into a woman's car: 'I can't believe a woman has hit my f***ing £40,000 car.' Now he can't harass, intimidate or abuse anyone in the county.

FAMILY MISFORTUNES

A family that prays together stays together. and these clans have sure lived by that rule. Just maybe this lot misheard 'prays' as 'affrays.'

ASTON'S VILLAINS BOOKED

Two brothers were given orders after
a 'mind your car, mister' style racket
outside Villa Park in Birmingham.
The teenagers, aged 15 and 14,
intimidated football fans watching
Aston Villa games out of money in
a racket that landed them up to
£3 a vehicle. In his defence, and
sounding like an old Cockney getting
misty-eyed about the Krays, one
of the brothers claimed that there
had been less vandalism under his

watch. The lads were banned from going near the stadium on match days, meaning that from now on Villa fans can sleep safely in their seats.

DOUBLE TROUBLE

Twin girls were each given orders by Huddersfield council to curb their behaviour, leading their 32-year-old mother to quip proudly 'they're the Asbo twins.' The 15-year-olds had been accused of smoking dope, assault, abuse and terrifying neighbours. Mummy protested that the pair were being 'victimised.'

EAST ANGLIA'S DIRTY DOZEN

A 41-year-old received Suffolk's first Asbo after frequent complaints about loud music. But after damage to their property and to others, nuisance from the kids, loud music, abuse and threats to neighbours, eventually the housing association lost patience and kicked her – and 11 other residents – out of the 7-bedroom house. In a hugely original defence. the woman said she was being 'victimised' and added 'I'm not a violent person anymore', just the sort of statement that will of course bring great comfort to whoever's unlucky enough to next share a street with her.

FORGET 50c. MEET 50 INCHES

For any aspiring villain there are two golden rules to always live by — never be a grass and love your mum to a sickeningly sentimental degree. Which must have confused a particular 11-year-old, whose own mum requested he be given an Asbo for behaviour that ranged from smashing property to GBH. The 4ft 2in Nottingham lad even went out boozing and after one especially titanic session, was brought home drunk by police when most of his contemporaries were already tucked up in their pyjamas.

MR, MRS & MASTER ASBO

A father-of-five in Crawley is facing

jail after he breached an Asbo preventing him from using abusive language, obscene gestures and intimidating his elderly neighbours. And while his son also received one, the woman of the household had to go to court for failing to keep their pet Rottweiler under control.

FAMILY VALUES

Two teenagers, 17 and 14 respectively and Leicester's biggest tearaways, were banned from a nearby district for two years, but they are unlikely to get a telling off from mum – because she's also been banned from the neighbourhood. So, no more shouting abuse, playing with fireworks or associating with other ne'er do wells for the Waltons of the East Midlands. The two boys also became the first kids in Leicester to have their names printed and distributed on leaflets as part of the city council's policy of naming and shaming.

BANNED OF BROTHERS

Two sets of Brummie brothers were part of a seven-strong teenaged gang given Asbos for extortion, abusive behaviour, racist language, and taunting a mother about her six-year-old daughter's terminal illness. All received Asbos of up to three years and night-time curfews. So horrendous were their actions that in this case even the mandatory mum-defending-little-angel-and-claiming-victimisation quote couldn't be obtained by any journalist.

7 YEARS OF BAD LUCK FOR SHOPS

Having a good woman is meant to keep you on right track, but not for one 34-year-old. The Middlesex drug-addict is banned from entering any shop in the whole of England or Wales with his girlfriend after a seven-year stealing spree. On the bright side, this is usually about the right length of time for the itch to turn a relationship sour.

ASBO RECORDS

In the world of low-level criminality, here profiled are Britain's youngest, oldest, most prolific and drunkest Asboites.

YOUNGEST FEMALE

The award for the youngest female
Asbo goes to an 11-year-old in
Hastings, who received an order
this summer barring her from
hurling eggs and stones, spitting
and rampaging through gardens.
The 4ft 3in girl is a veritable little
bundle of crime, and has also
been suspended from school for
smashing windows. But it's all going
to change now: she says she's given
up smoking, although still has the

odd swig of Stella from time to time.
Her heavily tattooed mother has been
served with a parenting order and
admits her daughter 'is no angel',
possibly the biggest understatement
since Emperor Hirohito said the
war 'isn't going necessarily to our
advantage' after two of Japan's
cities had been vaporised. And
in what can only be considered a
coup for the tourist board of the
depressed Sussex town, she lives
very close to Britain's youngest

disqualified driver. a 12-year-old boy.

LONGEST

Two women received the longest
ever Asbos after turning their
council house into a crack den.
The Brummie pair were evicted
and given orders to stay away
from their house for ten years.

IRELAND'S BEST

Northern Ireland has been slow to

take up the correction of miscreants by Asbos, a job that has traditionally been left to the IRA and its more 'direct action' approach. The first adult disorderly in the province is a 22-year-old man from Belfast, who is forbidden from playing loud music in his flat at any time, and from having more than three people in his home between midnight and 8am.

DRUNKEST

The first person banned from

drinking in England and Wales (in December 2002) is now on the run three years later. Last year the Cheltenham man breached his order by behaving aggressively. after forcing a petrol station assistant to turn on the pump – she refused because his friend was smoking at the time. Though newspaper reports weren't sure whether he wanted it for his car or to take away the pain. finding an alcoholic in booze-mad Britain will be no easy task for police.

MOST COMPLAINTS

A 16-year-old chalked up 400 reported anti-social incidents, the highest on record – and all within a prolific six-month period. The gang leader from Gloucestershire was responsible for hurling eggs, overturning dustbins and stone-throwing, as well as the usual threats and intimidation, and he notched up an Asbo record double by having every single householder in one street complain about him.

Meanwhile one of his side-kicks even set off a rape alarm in the face of a heart attack victim; times have changed since the days of Beano-style youthful misdemeanours.

OLDEST FEMALE

You're never too old: a 74-year-old is Britain's oldest female Asbo recipient, after 20 years of making life unpleasant for all around her. The former teacher from Lancashire was sending poison-pen letters to the council accusing neighbours of benefit fraud, playing deafening music, and shouting obscenities to passers-by, calling one a 'child molester', a hapless woman 'prostitute' and 'whore', and shouting 'slag' to a passing 13-year-old girl.

MOST BREACHES

A 15-year-old from Macclesfield holds the record for breaking his Asbo eight times in a year, and seven of these within a memorable five-week spell (most of the rest

of the 12 months were spent in
a young offender institute). The
schoolboy has 11 convictions for 34
offences. a fairly decent batting
average even for the standards of
today's teenage prison-fodder.

FIRST MOTORISED

A car thief became the first individual
banned from any car park in his
area. although at least he'll never
get lost in some place called the
blue zone. section 4 after an epic

shopping spree. The Middlesbrough 24-year-old was also prohibited from wearing baseball caps or hooded tops until 2006, allowing him to save up for next season's line of market stall 'Kelvin Klune' knock-offs.

HIGHEST ASBO DENSITY

A council estate in West Gorton, Manchester, has the dubious honour of holding the record for the highest number of Asbos among its inhabitants. The district, setting for

the funny-but-depressing TV show
Shameless, also has the lowest life
expectancy in England; it would hold
that record for the whole UK were it
not for Glaswegians and their love of
booze, fags and deep-fried heroin.

YOUNGEST SIBLINGS

The youngest brothers to be awarded
Asbos are twins aged ten years
old, and their 13-year-old brother
made it a hat-trick for the Great
Yarmouth family. The pair's behaviour

ranged from the usual fighting, swearing and abuse, to using a ball-bearing gun to take shots at passing cars and neighbours' windows.

OLDEST

And finally, Liverpool is home to the oldest owner of an Asbo, who, at 88, had been on the losing side of a ten-year battle with neighbours, police and – by the sounds of it – sanity. The order banned the great-grandfather from banging doors and bin lids, filming neighbours, using other people's driveways or making sarcastic comments. He had even kept samples of spit and crap allegedly left on his garage door. Although he breached the order and should have gone to jail, the bleeding heart liberal of a judge could see no sense in locking up the deaf octogenarian.

PROBLEMS WITH ASBOS

NOT EVERYONE IS PLEASED
WITH THE NEW LAW:

A Mori poll in June showed that while
89% of people supported Asbos, only

39% thought them to be effective.

Some say they are not deterrent
enough: 42% were breached by
December 2003. and of those
who breached them. less than
half got prison sentences.

According to the Institute for Brain-
Injured Children. at least five autistic
people have been given Asbos.

Although they cost an average

of £5,350, some Asbos take as much as £100,000 out of council coffers, with the highest so far having cost £187,700 – in Manchester, unsurprisingly.

The Council of Europe's human rights commissioner, Alvaro Gil-Robles, has criticised them – the last country to get a ticking off was Russia – and even said Britain was in the grips of 'Asbomania.'

Asbo Concern, a civil liberties
group, has been formed to
fight their over-use.

A 15-year-old schoolboy in Richmond,
Surrey, won a court battle to overturn
a local curfew, and was backed by
the human rights group Liberty. The
kid, who himself has never been in
trouble, said the ban – that stopped
him and everyone else his age from
going out between 9pm and 6am
– breached his human rights. Gone

are the day when boys his age would be happy with a day off from the mill every month and a shiny penny for their hard labour.

But the biggest worry is that, as well as targeting the lager-swilling amateur mechanic with a penchant for swearing at the neighbour's kids, the orders are being used against people who are just a little odd. To quote limp-wristed funnyman Julian Clary, 'The

English like eccentrics. They just
don't like them living next door.

THE WEIRD AND NOT SO WONDERFUL

Just to prove that Britain is a nation not only of oddballs proud of their freedom, but of interfering busybodies desperate to get rid

of that same liberty. here are
some of the stranger Asbos
that have been dished out.

HAM-FISTED ARREST

A Norfolk farmer received the
unusual (and unwanted) first Asbo
issued for uncontrollable livestock
after his pigs ran amok several
times in surrounding properties.
The 62-year-old was arrested
a day later after the anti-social
hogs breached the order. but had

charges dropped after receiving support from as far as Australia.

BOY IN THE HOOD

A lad in Cheetham, Manchester, was banned from wearing a hooded top for five years after a three-year long campaign of terror – and way before everyone got on the anti-hoodie bandwagon. The high-spirited 16-year-old had thrown fireworks at one cyclist and had grabbed another while threatening him with an axe. As well as the ban on wearing a hoodie or cap in public, he can't enter most of the Collyhurst district, is unable to congregate with more than two people, and can no longer possess fireworks, axes or chainsaws. Boys and their little toys, they just never grow up do they?

MOTOR CITY MADNESS

While Birmingham was once the proud home of Britain's mighty car industry, these days it's pretty much been reduced to a pair of amateur enthusiasts in Kingstanding. But earlier this year the couple was ordered to stop carrying out car repairs after they turned their drive into 'a salvage yard.' Meanwhile across town in Chelmsley Wood. a 36-year-old man was awarded an Asbo that brought to an end a reign of slamming doors loudly.

A RIGHT CARRY ON

Grumpy neighbours in East Kilbride
got a 27-year-old woman an Asbo
stopping her from answering the door
or gardening in skimpy underwear.
Her defence that it was a hot day
held no sway with magistrates in
sunny Lanarkshire. Still, the ban
also covered shouting, swearing, and
letting friends use her garden as
a toilet, so it's not quite the Barbara
Windsor versus stern matron Carry
On affair the main accusation implies.

More disturbingly, another woman only just avoided an Asbo after stripping off and exposing herself to neighbours. The 73-year-old was given a community order instead.

MUSIC DON'T IMPRESS NEIGHBOURS MUCH

A man in Birmingham (yet again) had to give up his stereo after it disturbed his neighbours in up-market Edgbaston – with Shania Twain songs. One case where naming and shaming really would work.

BIRD BRAINS #1

Town councillors threatened two elderly women with orders if they did not refrain from feeding pigeons in Trowbridge. Wiltshire. The birds' droppings have cost thousands of pounds in damage. and the persistent feeding ruined plans to build a pigeon loft to concentrate the flying rats.

NO WATER FOR BATH LADY

A Bath woman has been banned from going into rivers or canals, or onto railway lines, after four failed suicide attempts brought out the emergency services. The Avon lady was given a 12-month conditional discharge and a two-year Asbo after her last attempt, and the order also prevents her from loitering on bridges or entering multi-storey car parks alone. To be fair to the woman, on the second occasion she did plead

with her rescuers to leave her alone.
But the magistrate ordered: 'You are
not to dip one toe, not one finger, in
a river or canal.' Perhaps if prison
fails to stop her, only the ultimate
deterrent of capital punishment
will end her reign of terror.

SLIM SHADY FAN RAPPED

Likewise, and once more in England's
second city, a 33-year-old female
devotee of Eminem and Dido
had thousands of pounds worth

of CDs and a karaoke machine
confiscated after driving neighbours
demented with loud music: in fact
so loud that it registered the same
decibel levels as a moving train.
and caused furniture next door
to move. She was finally banned
from owning a stereo, radio or TV.

VAN MAN GOT BAN

A Bristol publican thought his troubles
were over after his Asbo – for
putting up a sign saying 'porking

yard' in his pub's car park. Apparently the sign in the St. Judes area was deemed offensive to Muslims at a nearby mosque, and also to prudes worried it may refer to immoral behaviour (when surely pub car parks are for fighting?). But the 43-year-old got in trouble again this year after opening a burger van in the same car park – called the Asbo Snack Bar.

HOLE IN THE BRAIN GANG

A 19-year-old in Oldham is

banned from having the name of his gang shaved into his head. Did our ancestors fight for the Magna Carta in vain?

TOO OLD FOR THIS # 1

When police found a certain Southport gentleman in charge of a mobile phone. the 37-year-old was doomed to end up back in court. The chap has an order preventing him from possessing a pay-as-you-go mobile after making a string of prank calls to the emergency services – and nor can he incite others to do the same.

BIRD BRAINS # 2

A woman from the Kingdom of Fife was threatened with an Asbo by her local council after feeding our feathered friends in her garden, with one local comparing her back yard to Alfred Hitchcock's The Birds. The 60-year-old is vowing to fight the order. What is it with old women and birds?

IT'S A FAKE COP, GUV

A persistent burglar in London was banned from knocking on any doors, or phoning people without permission, after stealing from 250 elderly people while posing as a policeman and a milkman.

FLY GUY SHOT DOWN

Whatever one's social standing, the long arm of the Asbo is never far away. A managing director of a

£10m company received an Asbo from a district judge at Highbury Magistrates. His firm, a large flyposter company, was the scourge of Asbo-lovin' Camden Council, who were spending £250,000 a year cleaning up flyposter-related mess.

ILL BEHAVIOUR

A 53-year-old with a strange obsession with medical equipment has been banned from all NHS buildings in England and Wales. The

York man has been stealing them for 16 years, even faking a heart attack on one occasion just so he could get into an operating theatre. In the last year of his obsessive quest, he tried to acquire a surgical mask on no fewer than 47 separate occasions.

NOW *THAT'S* BINGE DRINKING

A 36-year-old Teeside man was banned from entering any garage forecourt, after his runaway alcohol problem meant the local brew just wasn't doing it for him.

SOAP BLAMED FOR ROW

A couple arrested for an argument came up with the perfectly logical explanation, just days after receiving an Asbo for noise. The pair from Alloa claimed the sound was coming from the TV – possible, bearing in mind they were apparently watching Eastenders at the time. And since their Asbo banned them from stereo and not television abuse,

there's nothing wrong with watching
a good soap row involving words
like 'muppet', 'slag' and 'cow.'

TOO OLD FOR THIS # 2

A woman with a paranoid personality
disorder was given a whopping six-
year order after attacking her brother
with a rhubarb. The 50-year-old
from North Yorkshire flew into a rage
after her 72-year-old brother laughed
at her while he reversed his Land
Rover down a lane. She hurled three

sticks of the vegetable at her sibling, one of which landed in his right eye and left him with double vision.

SO REMEMBER, LOVE THY NEIGHBOUR

And just once more to show that every time an Englishman opens his mouth, another instantly hates him: A grandfather of 82 was banned from playing his TV or radio at top volume, as part of a long-running battle with his disabled neighbour.

The Asboite said in his defence that it was only done to drown out the sound of his rival's singing. 'The worst song was Jumpin' Jack Flash, but Ten Green Bottles and Cockles and Mussels were bad too,' he said. And just for good measure, his 55-year-old son also received an order.

GET SOMEONE ASBOED!

Sick of your boring uncle and auntie inviting themselves around for Boxing Day? Tired of your boss's lame jokes? Bored by your friend's pub anecdotes about hugely exaggerated pulling and fighting incidents? Get them barred from your presence, stuck in their house at night or banned from anything but saintly behaviour. With Asbos rising at the current rate, soon they will be so fashionable that no one should be without at least one.

If you want to get someone Asboed, don't call 999 – you'll only find yourself in next year's newspaper run about stupid emergency calls, along with some idiot asking for a good curry house. Asbos are dealt with by local authorities, not the police.

Most local councils in England will have an Asbo unit directly responsible for dealing with complaints. Birmingham, for example, has a team of 16 and received 10,000 calls last year, leading to 184 Asbos. Look up your local council and find the right department.

Firstly you must convince the authorities that your chosen enemy's behaviour 'blights the quality of community life' and that they are 'unreasonable.' So it's not enough that they're acting selfishly, it has to be beyond the standard norms of society — which doesn't include people failing to get their round or family sending unwanted annual round robins. And if the council thinks you are in danger of violence, they will fast-track proceedings.

You'd also be advised to make a
diary, detailing all the nasty things
they've ever done, from snubbing
your morning nod to trying to kill
your dog. This may get presented
to the council, so don't mix it up
with personal feelings of love,
soppy poetry or an office 'hit list.'

It helps if someone else also has the
same grudge – a multiple complaint
against an individual will stick
quicker, though do not consult too

closely: at least one case has fallen to pieces because the neighbours' stories matched too closely.

But be prepared for a little comeback – the cloak of anonymity is not as strong as in criminal cases and some complainants have been issued with personal alarms. So make sure it's done to someone with a sense of humour.

AND FINALLY...

A man compiling a list of dog's names in Hull came across the latest must-have pooch moniker – Asbo. Ian Killen was collecting the names for a tea towel to commemorate Hull's literature festival in May this year when he heard the Staffordshire bull terrier being called by its master. So whatever the merits of the Asbo, it has become as much a part of noughties Britain as Anglo-French squabbles, hoodie hysteria and ill-advised midriffs on women. And who knows – it may even replace Fido one day.

Note on the author

Ed West writes for Nuts and lives in London where he spends most of his time drinking lager in his garden while dressed only in his underpants. threatening to kill his next-door neighbours. and blaming the council for victimising him.

If you enjoyed this book, then you're going to love the following...

The Little Book of Stupid Drunks
1-905102-23-2
£2.99

the little eBay book

UNOFFICIAL   UNOFFICIAL

The website's most weird and wondrous...

The Little eBay Book
1-905102-19-4
£2.99

The Little Book of Pervs
1-905102-38-0
£2.99

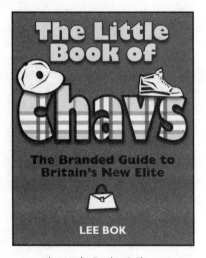

The Little Book of Chavs

The Branded Guide to Britain's New Elite

LEE BOK

The Little Book of Chavs
1-905102-01-1
£2.99

The Little Book of Students
1-905102-26-7
£2.99

All Crombie Jardine books are available
from your High Street bookshops.
Amazon. Littlehampton Book Services.
or Bookpost (P.O.Box 29, Douglas,
Isle of Man, IM99 1BQ.
tel: 01624 677 237. email: bookshop@
enterprise.net. Free postage and
packing within the UK).

If you have any comments or suggestions
for other Little Books, please e-mail us:
imayob@crombiejardine.com

www.crombiejardine.com